THE STA... ...IBRARY

PREHISTORIC ANIMALS

General Editors:
MICHAEL W. DEMPSEY
AND ANGELA SHEEHAN

Published by the World Publishing Company.
First American Edition 1970.
Library of Congress Catalog Card Number 75-128527
© 1970 Macdonald and Company (Publishers) Ltd.
Printed in Great Britain

THE WORLD PUBLISHING COMPANY
NEW YORK AND CLEVELAND

Many millions of years ago, the world was an empty place. There were no plants. There were no animals. There were no people.

After a long time, there were plants and animals living in the sea. Millions of years later, other plants and animals lived on the land.

The pictures show some of the animals that once lived on the Earth.

skeleton of
Iguanodon

Prehistoric animals lived on the Earth long before there were people.

We know about prehistoric animals because their bones turned to stone after they died. These bones can now be found in rocks. They are called fossils.

Scientists put the bones together so that people can see what prehistoric animals looked like.

Fossils of small animals are often found in rocks. Many are shells of animals that once lived in the sea.

fossil shell

The first animals lived in the sea. Some were like the animals that live in the sea today. Jellyfish floated in the water. Worms lived in the mud at the bottom.

There were also tiny animals called trilobites. They lived at the bottom of the sea and dug in the mud for food. When it was frightened, the trilobite could curl up into a ball.

The first fish had no jaws. Their bodies were covered with bony scales. The scales protected them like a suit of armor.

This fish came later. It was as large as an elephant. It had strong jaws and ate other fish.

This fish was one of the first sharks. All the bones in its body were soft.

This fish was like many fish which live in the sea today. It had hard bones. It also had an air sac in its body which helped it to float.

As time passed, less and less rain fell. Big rivers turned into muddy pools and many fish died. But some fish could breathe out of water. They also had strong fins which they could use to propel themselves. These fish crawled out of the water and began to live on the land.

The fish living on the land slowly changed. Their fins grew into legs. Their tails grew longer. Their heads became big and bony.

These were the first amphibians. Amphibians are animals which spend most of their life on land. They go back to water to lay their eggs.

early amphibian

RobinSon

Eryops

Some amphibians grew very big. Eryops was as long as a crocodile. It could not run fast, but Eryops had strong jaws to defend itself.

fossil of Eryops

strong jaws

There was a small frog-like amphibian called Miobatrachus.

The largest amphibian was bigger than a crocodile. It is called Eogyrinus.

Miobatrachus

Eogyrinus

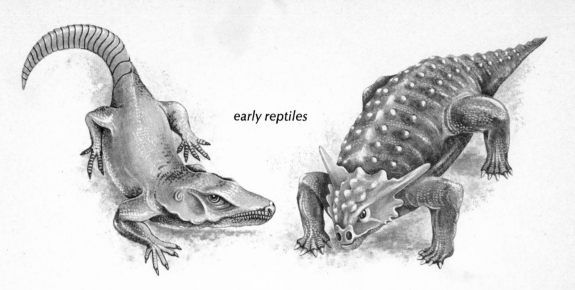

early reptiles

After millions of years, some amphibians began to grow big scales on their bodies. Their eggs developed hard shells and could be laid on land. These animals were the first reptiles.

Dimetrodon

Some prehistoric reptiles looked like animals which live today.

One looked like a turtle with a long, spiky tail.

One looked like a crocodile with a long snout.

One reptile had wings made of skin. This reptile did not flap its wings. It lived in trees and glided from one tree to another.

The biggest reptiles were the dinosaurs. Stegosaurus was an armored dinosaur. It had bony flaps on its back and big spikes on its tail. Stegosaurus looked fierce, but it ate only plants. When it was attacked, Stegosaurus swung its spiked tail like a club.

Stegosaurus

Brontosaurus was as big as ten elephants. Brontosaurus was so heavy that it could not stand for long on land. It spent most of the time in lakes, where the water helped to support its body. Brontosaurus needed so much food that it ate plants all day long.

Brontosaurus

Many dinosaurs were peaceful plant eaters. Their enemies were the meat-eating dinosaurs. The biggest meat eater was the terrible Tyrannosaurus. It had huge jaws with long jagged teeth.

Some animals could run fast enough to escape from Tyrannosaurus. Some had bony armor which helped to protect them.

Triceratops

Tyrannosaurus

Robinson

Not all of the reptiles lived on land. There were reptiles flying in the air and swimming in the sea.

Flying reptiles had wings made of skin. Pteranodon had wings bigger than any bird has today. It could glide over the sea for days, looking for food. It had a long beak. When it saw a fish, Pteranodon swooped down and snatched it out of the water.

In the sea there were giant reptiles such as Plesiosaurus. Their necks were as long as their bodies. Their long necks made it easy for them to catch fish.

Pteranodon

Plesiosaurus

21

Archaeopteryx

While the great dinosaurs ruled the land, the first bird with feathers flew in the air. Its wings were weak and it could not fly very well.

The first bird was called Archaeopteryx. A fossil has been found which shows just how this bird looked.

Archaeopteryx was the size of a crow. It had feathers on its wings like the birds living today. It had teeth in its beak like the flying reptiles which lived at that time.

fossil of Archaeopteryx

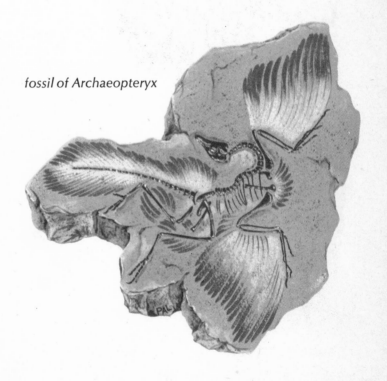

While the last of the dinosaurs still lived, there were small furry animals running about. They were so small that the dinosaurs did not bother to eat them.

The furry animals were the first mammals. They looked like rats. They ate eggs and insects.

When the dinosaurs died out, mammals grew larger. There were sloths as tall as trees and pigs as big as donkeys.

Eohippus

four toes

The first horse had four toes on its front feet and three toes on its back feet.

Millions of years later, horses had three toes on each foot. The middle toe was the biggest.

Today, horses have one toe on each foot. It is called a hoof.

Merychippus

three toes

modern horse

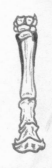

one toe

About a million years ago, the world grew very cold. Much of the land was covered with ice.

The Great Ice Age had begun.

Only animals like the mammoth were able to live in the

warm. Other animals moved to warmer parts of the world.

Mammoths have been found frozen in ice. The ice has preserved them for thousands of years. The freezer of a refrigerator preserves food in the same way.

Mammoth

After many thousands of years, the world gradually grew warmer and most of the ice melted. By this time, there was a new creature living on the Earth. It was man.

Man was much smaller than many of the animals which lived at that time. But he was smarter than any of them.

He built fires to frighten away the wild animals. He made spears and hunted the mammoth for food.

The saber-toothed tiger was an enemy of prehistoric man. This fierce animal had big dagger-like teeth. Man used his spears to fight the saber-toothed tiger.

Dimetrodon

Tyrannosaurus

PREHISTORIC ANIMALS
COMPARED IN SIZE
WITH MAN.

Man

Pteranodon

Mammoth

Brontosaurus